THE MANAGING CUSTOMER SERVICE POCKETBOOK

By Andy Cross

Drawings by Phil Hailstone

"Great businesses make customer service [   ]rgin we invest time in helping our people and es[   ]e the brilliant service that our customers expect. [   ]r the daily team meetings or developing a long-term plan for [   ], this guide provides a wealth of knowledge and ideas to make it a reality."
Michael Murphy, Group Brand Manager – Customer Service, Virgin Management Limited

"When it comes to delivering excellent service, it's turning great ideas into practical actions that makes the noticeable difference to business – and customers. This pocketbook will fire your enthusiasm to do more for your customers – starting today."
Sionade Robinson, Author, Researcher and Educator, Cass Business School

Published by:
Management Pocketbooks Ltd
Laurel House, Station Approach, Alresford, Hants SO24 9JH, U.K.
Tel: +44 (0)1962 735573 Fax: +44 (0)1962 733637
E-mail: sales@pocketbook.co.uk
Website: www.pocketbook.co.uk

This edition published 2008.

© Andy Cross 2008.

British Library Cataloguing-in-Publication Data – A catalogue record for this book is available
from the British Library.

ISBN 978 1 903776 92 6

Design, typesetting and graphics by **efex ltd**. Printed in U.K.

CONTENTS

INTRODUCTION 7
The critical difference, how to use
this book, build a service brand,
customer trends, trend spotting

BUILD A CUSTOMER 17
SERVICE BRAND
Bottom line difference, be exceptional,
hitting growth and profitability targets,
beyond satisfaction, creating loyalty,
winning hearts, minds and hands, love
to work, what drives engagement, fill
in the blanks, pub sentence, grab a
notepad, every link in the chain

SET THE CHALLENGE 37
TO YOUR PEOPLE
Set the bar high, what customers
really really want!, getting the right
things right, flicking the switch, quality
factors, loyalty building experiences,
let's be friends, customers are
individuals, magic touches

PUT THE CUSTOMER 53
AT THE HEART
What must you do, set the recruitment
bar high, on the training ground, shared
values, balanced measures, recognition
and reward, community service

COACH FOR BRILLIANT SERVICE 67
Flattening the pyramid, freedom to act,
gift of feedback, customer contact, when
performance falters, getting your people
together, off to a flying start, wrap it up,
fantastic story teller, passing the ball,
every touch matters, turnaround, positive
mental attitude, Polaroid picture

CREATE THE FREEDOM 93
TO IMPROVE
Bounce back, customer charter,
customer feedback, putting on the ears,
feedback methods, one step beyond,
mystery shoppers, competitors, what if…?,
inside the customer's head, keep moving

THANKS FROM THE AUTHOR

In my work I have read widely and been influenced by many great people. There is a list of excellent books at the back which I thoroughly recommend. My apologies if I haven't accurately referenced where other people have directly influenced what I have written.

Several people have helped me get this book ready for you to read, some have inspired me and others have given me the time and space to think.

Special thanks to:

Sionade Robinson	**Paul Tizzard**	**Erica Reeves**
Lyn Etherington	**Michael Murphy**	**Kirstie Moon**
Richard Lowe	**Frank Dick**	**Adela Cross**

MANAGING CUSTOMER SERVICE

FOREWORD

SOME WORDS FROM FRANK DICK, OBE

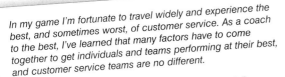

In my game I'm fortunate to travel widely and experience the best, and sometimes worst, of customer service. As a coach to the best, I've learned that many factors have to come together to get individuals and teams performing at their best, and customer service teams are no different.

*Importantly, you also have to be good at your own 3 Rs; **responsibility** for your own performance, **responsibility** for your own development and **responsibility** for coaching others. In this book Andy has pulled together some great ideas to help you focus on the 3 Rs so that you can create an organisation where your people have the ability, fitness and mindset to provide excellent customer service, time after time.*

Good luck and keep smiling, Frank

Coaching has been Frank's raison d'être for decades, inspiring world-beating performances from some of the top names in sport – Daley Thompson, Boris Becker, Gerhard Berger, Denise Lewis, Marat Safin and Katarina Witt. In business, he has helped develop a coaching culture in Barclays, BT, Unilever, Shell, Abbey and Rolls Royce.

ABOUT THE AUTHOR

Andy is Head of Organisation & People Development at Virgin Atlantic. This book is, without doubt, influenced by his experience working for an organisation with such a powerful brand and reputation for exceptional service. That said, this book is not about Virgin or, indeed, a detailed account of how the airline has achieved its results.

The ideas have been drawn from a variety of sources, organisations and, of course, the author's own hands-on experience delivering customer service that started many years ago on a fruit and vegetable market stall in East Anglia!

INTRODUCTION

INTRODUCTION

THE CRITICAL DIFFERENCE

Thank you for making the decision to open this book. It is written in the belief that excellent customer service really can make a critical difference to the success or failure of your organisation. Get it right consistently and you will turn satisfied customers into loyal advocates, the kind of people who are walking, talking PR machines for what you do. Get it wrong and handle complaints poorly, and you will create people willing to eat away at your reputation and you'll never even know that it is happening.

Many organisations invest significant time, money and effort in finding new customers but fail to pay at least equal attention to keeping the customers they already have – what a waste!

As someone responsible for managing customer service, your challenge is to achieve excellent customer service **through other people**. This book contains a collection of ideas, new and old, that will help you create a passion for service in those around you.

Enjoy!

HOW TO USE THIS BOOK

Customers are not perfect. All are different, some have unrealistic expectations, and many change their minds and, often, make rash emotional decisions.

Our customers are only human!

As a manager, you have the added challenge of delivering a service using humans! Your people are just as unpredictable as your customers. And then you can add yourself into the equation and, despite popular belief, you are only human too.

Your biggest challenge is to bring together all of this unpredictability in a way that delights your customer, time after time.

BUILD A SERVICE BRAND

In this book we share ideas, new and old, to help you, the person leading customer service, navigate your way to success. We start in the next chapter with the concept of building a **service brand**. The following chapters, in turn, take you through what **you** can do to achieve this.

You will **set the challenge** to your people to deliver the standards that make a real difference to your customer.

You will **put the customer at the heart** of everything that you do.

You will **coach for brilliant service** to your customers.

You will **create the freedom to improve** so that you delight your customers even more.

BUILD A SERVICE BRAND

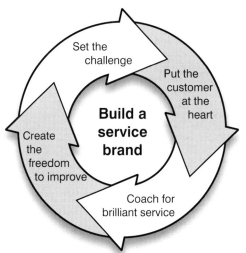

CUSTOMER TRENDS

We live in a rapidly changing world which, in turn, drives subtle changes in the people around us. The first challenge is to keep ahead or, at least, keep up with the change in your customers. Here are some examples of the changes you can currently observe and how you could make the most of the opportunity.

Trend	**Question**
The pace of life is getting quicker	How can you build relationships in a hurry?
People like the self-esteem of passing on personal recommendations	How can you build that level of friendship with your customers?
You can no longer trust the media	How can you reinforce the honesty of your dealings with customers?

CUSTOMER TRENDS

Trend	**Question**
Good manners are increasingly rare	How do your people display excellent manners?
People get stressed by too much choice	How can you better guide people through the decision-making process?
Ethics and morals are more important to people	What can you do to make your values clear and, importantly, match those of your customers?

A good example of how a company has embraced the trend of time and technology is the call back facility that Amazon has on their website. You click a button and your phone will ring with a real person on the line ready to help. No queues, no menu options!

Acknowledgements to Sionade Robinson & Lyn Etherington

TREND SPOTTING

Many organisations focus on product innovation and rely on 'futurists' to identify trends and opportunities. Innovation in service is equally important so, how do you become your own futurist? Here are some ideas to get you started.

- Read widely – magazines, internet, newspapers – and include media you wouldn't normally use but your customers might

- Notice what's going on around you and ask what it means to your organisation, eg what is changing in the high street? What are people spending their time doing?

- Watch TV, check out the internet and track blog sites – what's hot, what's not?

TREND SPOTTING

- Look outside your business – learn from competitors, other industries and other countries

- Ask your employees – especially people most like your customers, or more importantly, like your future customers

- Talk to your best customers

- Remember that you are a customer too – look at the way you act and react

Do today what others will not, so that you may do tomorrow what others cannot do.

NOTES

BUILD A CUSTOMER
SERVICE BRAND

A BOTTOM LINE DIFFERENCE

So, why all the fuss about building an organisation renowned for the quality of its customer service – a customer service brand? We all know that retaining an existing customer is usually much cheaper than finding a new customer, but did you know that:

 A 7% increase in word of mouth advocacy unlocks a 1% increase in company growth *(2005 study by the London School of Economics)*

 The same study showed that a 2% reduction in negative word of mouth boosts sales growth by 1%

 Xerox conducted a study which found that a 'highly satisfied' customer is six times more likely to buy again than one who is simply 'satisfied'

 The longer you keep your customer, the lower the amortised cost of acquiring that customer

 Loyal, longer-term customers are less inclined to switch and also tend to be less sensitive to price changes, resulting in more stable sales and making market entry harder for competitors

BE EXCEPTIONAL

Service that is good, but not exceptional, can be your worst enemy. The difference between 'OK' and 'exceptional' is the difference between a customer who *might* buy from you again and one who will *definitely* buy from you again…and again.

HITTING YOUR GROWTH AND PROFITABILITY TARGETS

Research indicates that the target of real business growth and profits is in your sights – the inner ring of the archery target.

And the best bit is that customers are human, so the price of your product or service is not everything; although value for money does help. As the research shows, you can make a difference without discounts, loss leaders and free gifts.

Building a customer service brand has to be one of your targets. This book will explore what you can do, as a customer service leader, to make the difference.

Let's take a look at the other rings of the target. What else needs to be in place to grow your business profitably?

BUILD A CUSTOMER SERVICE BRAND

BEYOND SATISFACTION

Customers expect to be satisfied. It is, after all, what they have paid you to deliver. If your customer service is really going to make a difference you have to aim even higher. Loyalty needs at least a 9 out of 10. If you want loyalty, you need to earn the customer's trust and confidence time and time again.

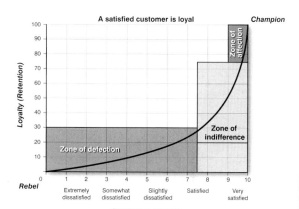

Adapted from *Beyond Customer Loyalty*, James L. Heskett, Managing Customer Quality Journal

CREATING LOYALTY

Imagine the customer on a spectrum that runs from *dissatisfied* through to *loyal*. If you are going to create loyalty you have to deliver the basics brilliantly, and more. As the diagram on the next page shows, once you have achieved this level of performance you have more than a customer, you have a champion – someone who comes back for more and brings friends with them.

CREATING LOYALTY

Similarly, if you over-promise or fail to deliver consistently, then you have a real business issue on your hands, with the hard work of your sales and marketing teams being reversed by an undercover rebel working for your competition – free of charge!

Dissatisfaction	Satisfaction	Loyalty
Fail to deliver	Deliver what you promise; the basics	Deliver the basics brilliantly and do more than expected
Rebel	**Indifferent**	**Champion**
Will leave you and, through negative word of mouth, will take existing customers with them and prevent others from ever trying you!	Waiting to be delighted by you, wooed by your competitors or worse still turned into rebels	Will become less price sensitive and will forgive the occasional mistake if you handle it well. They will come back for more and bring friends with them.

(23)

WINNING HEARTS, MINDS AND HANDS

What is it that you have to do to deliver the exceptional service that builds loyalty? Well actually, *you* don't do anything for the customer – it's your people who deliver the customer service, or fail to.

Senior managers have two favourite clichés: '*our people are our greatest asset*' and '*if you keep your people happy your customers will be happy*'. In reality they are wise words, they just sound rather hollow when they are not backed up with action.

BUILD A CUSTOMER SERVICE BRAND

WINNING HEARTS, MINDS AND HANDS

If you treat your people well a few magical things will start to happen:

- Your people will put in the extra effort when it matters most
- They will have the confidence to be creative in how they meet customers' needs
- They will grow in experience, making them better able to deliver the service
- They will stick around longer, so strengthening the relationships they have with your customers
- Your people will feel free to innovate and improve how you do things
- They will motivate themselves and others to deliver an exceptional experience

In a phrase........**engage the hearts and minds of your people and you win the hands.**

Your people will consistently deliver the levels of service you need to shift mere customer satisfaction into the realms of loyalty.

Acknowledgements to the work of James L. Heskett, W. Earl Sasser Jr., Leonard A. Schlesinger; The Service Profit Chain. (25)

LOVE TO WORK

You have to get your people beyond happy and into *engaged*; you have to spread a little love – that's what drives performance.

So, the question is, *'how deep is the love?'*

Towers Perrin-ISR, employee research specialists, use a simple set of questions (see next page) to measure the extent to which your people are engaged and, therefore, likely to win the hearts and minds of your customers.

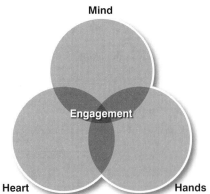

BUILD A CUSTOMER SERVICE BRAND

LOVE TO WORK
QUESTIONS

Here are some good questions to ask yourself and your people. Ask them in focus groups, individually or ideally as part of a more complete employee opinion survey.

Minds – what do I think about my organisation?	Hearts – how do I feel about my organisation?	Hands – what am I willing to do for my organisation?
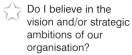 Do I believe in the vision and/or strategic ambitions of our organisation?	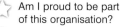 Am I proud to be part of this organisation?	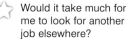 Would it take much for me to look for another job elsewhere?
 Do I share the values for which our organisation stands?	Would I recommend my organisation to my friends?	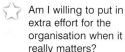 Am I willing to put in extra effort for the organisation when it really matters?

Listen carefully to whether your people talk about 'our' customers rather than 'the' customers!

Thanks to Towers Perrin-ISR. To find out more visit www.isrinsight.com

BUILD A CUSTOMER SERVICE BRAND

WHAT DRIVES ENGAGEMENT?

This is where you, the customer service manager, really make the difference.

- A reputation for customer service, a service brand, has the potential to make a difference to your bottom line

- Creating a service brand costs relatively little, certainly when compared to the cost of acquiring new customers or replacing those you lose through failing to create loyalty

- **Your people create the reputation for exceptional customer service**

- As the manager, you can have a positive impact on the engagement of your people

In the following chapters we will explore what it takes to engage your people and build a service brand, whether that service is delivered on the phone, face to face or via the internet and email.

DO YOU HAVE A SERVICE BRAND?

How would you describe your brand in terms of service? Do you have a reputation for distinct or excellent service? The following three activities are designed to help you put into words your current service brand.

1. Fill in the blanks.
2. Pub sentence.
3. Grab a notepad.

Complete the activities and then reflect on what you find out. You can do the activities with anyone – with customers or your team – either individually or in groups. It's often the similarities and differences that tell the story.

BUILD A CUSTOMER SERVICE BRAND

1: FILL IN THE BLANKS

Give everyone in your team a blank outline of your organisation's name, logo or product. Ask them to fill it in with the words that best describe your organisation at its best or, alternatively, its worst.

Review the completed images and agree:

- What are your apparent strengths?

- What similarities do you find?

- What concerns you?

- What do you stand for?

BUILD A CUSTOMER SERVICE BRAND

2: PUB SENTENCE

Richard Branson says that if he is waiting at the bar to be served and a customer (existing or future) asks, '*what is the point of Virgin X?*' he should be able to answer them in a simple sentence. It's a great way to test if what you offer your customers is clear enough.

What answer would you give for your organisation?

How does your answer compare to what you already have formally written down in your organisation, ie your vision statement, your values and your product descriptions?

Are they different? What do you need to do to close the gap?

3: GRAB A NOTEPAD

If a customer came into contact with your organisation and your company name was blanked out, would they know it was you?

Grab a notepad and do some research at the key contact points with your customers – imagine you are the customer and write down what you notice. Here are some examples:

Website

- It took 6 clicks and 5 minutes to find a telephone number for existing customers but new customers get pop-ups in seconds.
- The information customers are likely to be searching for, eg directions and opening hours, is not easily accessible
- The language is too technical and navigation is just list after list

Reception

- The receptionists carried on talking to a colleague for 10-20 seconds
- No smile and minimal conversation
- There were no chairs on which to wait
- I was not told how long I would have to wait to be seen

3: GRAB A NOTEPAD

Other areas to consider:

- When someone telephones your customer hotline what actually happens?
- Do they get a better service if they phone your sales department?
- What feelings do your standard letters evoke?
- What do you do to welcome your customers whenever they come into contact with your organisation?
- What is being said about your organisation on the internet?

You can use this informal research to describe your existing service brand and identify what you could do to make an immediate improvement to the customer experience.

Forget your vision, values and service procedures – the stuff that is written down. Based on your research, do you have a distinct brand of service or not?

EVERY LINK IN THE CHAIN

We all rely on others to deliver exceptional service – inside and outside both our team and our business. New technology, cheaper sources of labour and the desire to future-proof your organisation, by focusing on core businesses, all mean that reliance on others outside the traditional organisational boundaries is increasingly common.

Your partners and suppliers are likely to be in a position either to directly serve your customers, eg a contact centre or a courier company, or to provide a service that could significantly affect your ability to deliver your service, eg contract cleaning or supply of airline meals. Your partners will often wear your uniform, answer your phones or supply the 'ingredients' to create your product or service. So, you are asking your partners to:

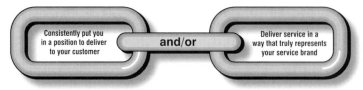

Consistently put you in a position to deliver to your customer

and/or

Deliver service in a way that truly represents your service brand

EVERY LINK IN THE CHAIN

Some ideas on how to demonstrate trust and respect towards your partners:

- Find partners who have complementary values to your own

- Encourage similar recruitment practices

- Agree common targets that go beyond the financial aspects

- Work in such a way that risks and rewards are shared

- Make your partners feel welcome in your workplace

- Create a sense of team with them

Continued...

BUILD A CUSTOMER SERVICE BRAND

EVERY LINK IN THE CHAIN

- Celebrate successes together
- Involve your partners in the 'essential' training for your people
- Openly share ideas about improving how you work together
- Share ideas about improving the customer experience
- Share customer feedback
- Get all your partners together to share your ambitions and generate ideas

Check out page 85 for more ideas on getting everyone to take responsibility for customer service.

Many companies will invite all existing partners together at least once a year to work on an agenda like the one above.

SET THE CHALLENGE
TO YOUR PEOPLE

SET THE CHALLENGE TO YOUR PEOPLE

SET THE BAR HIGH

One of your most important jobs is to champion the needs of your customer. What is the challenge you set for your people, on behalf of your customer?

In this chapter I will share some ideas to help you set the bar high.

WHAT CUSTOMERS REALLY, REALLY WANT!

The best way to understand your customers and meet their expectations is to ask them what they want! That said, there are some excellent frameworks to help you structure your thinking.

Zeithaml V.A. (*et al, 1992*) identified five keys (RATER) to satisfying customers, regardless of the service you are providing.

Reliability	Your ability to perform the service dependably and accurately
Assurance	Your employees' knowledge and courtesy, and their ability to inspire trust and confidence
Tangibles	Appearance of your physical facilities, equipment, personnel and communication materials
Empathy	The caring, individualised attention you give to your customers
Responsiveness	Your willingness to help customers, provide prompt service and solve problems

GETTING THE RIGHT THINGS RIGHT

You have many customers, each with slightly different, personal expectations. Trying to do everything right can be the downfall of even the most customer-focused team. So, how can you get the right things right?

Ask yourself, '*what is it that our customer truly values above all other things?*' Identify this and get it right again and again. For example:

Train operator – a level of reliability that underpins consistent punctuality
Retailer – tangible products on the shelf that provide an adequate choice
Security guards – the assurance that the company really cares about what it does
Insurer – empathy shown when handling claims
Airline – the non-negotiable assurance that safety comes first

It's sensible to explain to your people what really matters to your customers. It's absolutely paramount that you make sure that everyone understands what your customer values above everything else. **Never lose sight of this single aspect of your service**, regardless of what else you do.

FLICKING THE SWITCH

OK, you know what most customers want and what is singularly most important in your business. Did you know that you can turn your customers on and off in different ways? Here and on the next page are common examples of the quality factors that can switch your customers on and off.

Factors to turn your customers off (if missing)

Reliability
Integrity
Communication
Functionality
Competence

These are your basics, eg functionality (it must do what it says on the tin!). Get these factors wrong and you quickly turn your customers off you

What is your aim?
Deliver the basics as efficiently as possible. Investing extra effort here is unlikely to get your customers excited.

SET THE CHALLENGE TO YOUR PEOPLE

FLICKING THE SWITCH

Factors that can turn your customers on or off

Responsiveness
Care
Availability
Courtesy
} These factors have the ability to delight your customers but can also pitch them into darkness when missing

What is your aim? Deliver these basics brilliantly!

Factors to turn your customers on

Friendliness
Commitment
Attentiveness
Helpfulness
} The factors that delight your customers every step of the way

What is your aim?
If delighting your customer matters, invest in these areas!

Adapted from 'The determinants of service quality: satisfiers and dissatisfiers' Johnson 1995.

IDENTIFY YOUR QUALITY FACTORS

It's pretty straightforward to complete your own research to identify the quality factors that make a difference to your customers and, importantly, the effect they have on your customers.

Approach 1

Ask a range of your customers to describe particular incidents or transactions that have made them either very satisfied or dissatisfied with the service. Get them to describe the incident fully in their own words. Once complete you can 'code' the factors that appear to make a difference – good or otherwise.

Approach 2

Similar to approach 1, except you take a close look at your complaints and compliments. You can build this into your routine monitoring of customer communications. Remember, verbal feedback is just as important as written feedback, so do get your employees to pass this feedback onto you.

LOYALTY BUILDING EXPERIENCES

Research shows that it is possible to isolate what it actually is that impresses customers to the extent that it turns them into promoters. Robinson and Etherington identified eight loyalty building experiences.

Review your customer service and score each of these elements out of 10, with zero being very poor and 10 being exceptional.

Loyalty Building Experience	Score
1. It was easy to access someone who could help	
2. I spoke to a person who appeared/sounded positive and eager to help	
3. The person I spoke to listened well to what I had to say	
4. I felt that I had enough time and did not feel rushed	

SET THE CHALLENGE TO YOUR PEOPLE

LOYALTY BUILDING EXPERIENCES

5. I got a chance to ask any questions I had ☐

6. The person I spoke to seemed to have a good knowledge of what she/he was talking about ☐

7. The person I spoke to really gave me the impression that he/she enjoyed speaking to me ☐

8. The interaction was concluded to my complete satisfaction ☐

Total ☐

Adapted from Customer Loyalty: A guide for time travellers by Sionade Robinson & Lyn Etherington

LOYALTY BUILDING EXPERIENCES

RESULTS

0-40

Your honesty is compelling but your current levels of customer service are unlikely to match this. You have a great opportunity to make some quick and significant improvements that will drive your service brand.

41-72

You are doing some things well but it is likely that consistency is your challenge. Try revisiting your underlying processes and procedures to check they make it easy for your people to deliver loyalty building experiences. Also, check your approach to recruitment, training and coaching.

73+

Excellent! Your people probably give you a genuine competitive advantage over your competitors. Don't stand still, you have to keep innovating before the competition catch up!

LET'S BE FRIENDS

In his book, *The Loyalty Effect*, Frederick F. Reichheld talks about the willingness of your customers to recommend you to others as the true test of loyalty.

'Would you recommend this organisation to a friend, relative or colleague?'

Building on this belief, why don't you raise the bar even higher?

Friendships are incredibly powerful relationships, so what can you do to actually make your customers your friends? We do, after all, choose our friends, rely on them when times are tough and, within reasonable limits, cut them some slack when the relationship falters.

LET'S BE FRIENDS

What then do we expect from others if we are going to consider them friends?
Your list might include:

Honesty

Being there when it really matters

Confidence

Fun to be around

Friendliness

Keeping promises

Listening to what you have to say

What else would feature on your list?

How can you encourage your people
to develop these qualities when delivering
customer service?

SET THE CHALLENGE TO YOUR PEOPLE

CUSTOMERS ARE INDIVIDUALS

Some functions may talk about a *target audience* or *customer demographic*, eg males aged 16-24. It's absolutely vital that you don't let this thinking spill over into your customer service.

If you are to build loyalty, you must treat every customer as an individual. Wherever possible, encourage your people to speak from the heart, not a script. Talk to them about how they prefer to be talked to – with warmth and humanity. Real conversations will be more rewarding for everyone concerned! For example, if you work in a call centre and have someone who is clearly disgruntled, skip the up-selling script to avoid greater frustration. Similarly, if someone says it is their first time travelling to a new destination, then take the opportunity to share your own experience of that destination.

And if you get the chance to influence your marketing or finance people, at least ask them to imagine one real person who fits the target audience!

MAGIC TOUCHES

We've talked about the non-negotiable elements of your service – getting the right things right – the importance of efficiently delivering the basics. We've talked about getting beyond the basics into the realms of brilliant basics, eg shifting from friendliness (warmth, eye contact and smile) into friendship (first names, predicting needs, listening).

Beyond this come the moments you cannot plan, the little touches that mean so much to the customer and cost so little, where personality, freedom, confidence and care all come together.

A train manager took all of the placemats from the first class carriages and folded them into fans for the passengers caught in an unpleasantly hot carriage when the air conditioning failed.

An insurance clerk personally delivered a car insurance policy on the way home so that the customer was able to drive to an important meeting the next day.

SET THE CHALLENGE TO YOUR PEOPLE

MAGIC TOUCHES

As the manager, what is your role in creating magic touches?

It's about how you act, what you say and what you focus on before and after the magic touch!

 Let people know the boundaries of decision-making

 Give them the tools and information to get on with their jobs

 Make sure your people are really confident in their ability to deliver the basics

 Give them the freedom to try things out

 Measure the impact on the customer, not just the adherence to procedure

 Help people learn from mistakes when they happen

 Tell stories to get across the concept of magic

 Focus on what **can** be done….not what can't!

THE GIFT OF TIME

Just imagine if you had more time to spend on the things you really enjoy – what a luxury that would be in this busy world we live in. Our customers are just the same, so consider what you can do to give the gift of time.

- Design efficient processes to minimise the boring things, eg queues

- When you are asking someone to wait at home for a delivery, provide a specific time rather than the usual *am* or *pm* choice

- Get things right first time

- Don't put the customer on hold – take a number and call them back

- Get your customers to where they can start to enjoy the experience before you start asking questions, eg take them to their restaurant table

- Where possible, use the information you already hold about the customer rather than asking them time after time, eg when completing online forms

PUT THE CUSTOMER AT THE HEART

PUT THE CUSTOMER AT THE HEART

WHAT MUST YOU DO

In this section we will explore some of the 'must-do's' if you are successfully to put the customer at the heart of everything your organisation does. This will include subjects such as:

- Recruitment

- Training

- Vision and values

- Reward and recognition

- Community

PUT THE CUSTOMER AT THE HEART

SET THE RECRUITMENT BAR HIGH

Never take shortcuts when deciding who will join your team. A quick decision made simply to fill a vacancy will invariably backfire as you struggle to deliver the high standards your customer expects. Your people, through their personalities and expertise, will drive your service brand – **always recruit the best affordable person.**

Some ideas:

- Write job adverts and job descriptions that describe your service brand, expectations and even the customers

- Provide a realistic profile of the job before people have to decide if they want it. Watch carefully how candidates behave when they are not in the 'interview', and use your best people to help make the recruitment decision

- Unsuccessful, well-treated applicants could become future employees or customers. What do you do to treat them well? Vouchers? Personal letters? Constructive feedback?

Continued…

SET THE RECRUITMENT BAR HIGH

- Always know the attributes of your best people, eg highly organised, and ask potential employees for examples of occasions when they have displayed similar attributes

- If teamwork is important, set up a scheme where all your employees can be rewarded for recommending people who get hired. It can reduce advertising costs and people usually recommend candidates who will fit the team

- Encourage people you trust to 'talent spot' anyone who provides them with excellent customer service, eg in restaurants, shops, call centres. Provide a business card that contains contact details for your recruitment team

- Create a pool of people who really want to join your organisation – don't waste enthusiastic people just because you don't have a vacancy. If you are impressed by someone at interview, tell them – always give feedback – and encourage them to keep in touch or, better still, you keep in touch

- Treat hiring decisions as seriously as other financial investment decisions

PUT THE CUSTOMER AT THE HEART

ON THE TRAINING GROUND
INDUCTION TRAINING

You wouldn't send a player onto a pitch who didn't know the rules of the game or was too unfit to play. Let's look at the importance of induction, basic and refresher training.

Induction

All successful organisations have good induction training that covers health & safety, introductions, etc. If you want to put the customer at the heart of everything you do then it should feature loud and clear in your induction.

- Talk to new employees about your customers – who they are, the feedback they give when you get it right and what disappoints them
- Explain the promise you have made to the customer in terms of product, service and values
- Share your current business focus, how you measure success and your current targets
- Let them talk to your best people
- Invite your senior managers to talk to new recruits about the customer

ON THE TRAINING GROUND

BASIC TRAINING

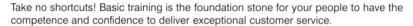

Take no shortcuts! Basic training is the foundation stone for your people to have the competence and confidence to deliver exceptional customer service.

- Customers expect your people to be knowledgeable so let them experience the product, eg a free meal in the restaurant, discounts on your clothes

- Make the training as real as possible so that new employees have the confidence to perform under pressure

- Weave your customer service messages throughout procedural and technical training

- Provide loads of real examples of great service provided by your people – tell your stories

ON THE TRAINING GROUND
BASIC TRAINING

- Let your new people put on the 'L' plates and learn in real, but supervised, situations, eg practise making (monitored) customer calls or working in the restaurant when it is quiet

- Buddy new people with your role model employees – let them be inspired by your best

- Make it clear what your 'non-negotiables' are for the customer

- Explain the decisions that the employee cannot make and then trust them to do the rest

- Polish the customer service skills that you observed at recruitment – help them shine!

ON THE TRAINING GROUND
REFRESHER TRAINING

Rules change, fitness levels drop and, as we all know, the customer always expects more. What do you do to keep your people fresh? Regularly get them together and provide the opportunity to:

- Share customer feedback

- Reinforce good habits and remove bad ones

- Ask your best people where the team needs a refresher

- Problem solve – listen to what makes the job difficult so you can act quickly to remove frustrations

- Collect ideas on how to improve the customer experience and act on the best

- Let people know what has changed

- Raise your standards every year…..because your competitors will

PUT THE CUSTOMER AT THE HEART

WHAT IS ON YOUR WALL?

Has your organisation invested in creating vision statements, company values and corporate scorecards? If so, you will probably find them on the wall – so take a close look to see how you can use them to reinforce the customer message. What does your vision statement say about the contribution you make to your customers?

Keeping dreams and ambitions alive when accident or illness strikes
(Insurance company)

Grow a profitable airline which people love to fly and where people love to work
(Airline)

We create peace of mind by delivering on time, every time, for all of our customers
(Distribution)

Powerful vision statements like these provide a great opportunity for people to understand that what they are doing really matters to the customer, especially if you link your key measures to the vision. Make sure your vision statement is visible at induction, and use it at team meetings to get people thinking about ideas to improve the customer experience.

SHARED VALUES

Your service brand is the promise you have made to your customers. Your ability to deliver that promise depends on the values your people have and, therefore, what they consistently do.

The greater the alignment between your brand values and the values of your employees, the easier it is to deliver your promise.

Use your company values wisely:

- Look for similar values at recruitment

- Ask your team to say which values they can relate to and why (and the reverse)

- Use your values as a way to brainstorm how you can show those values to your customer

- Put your values at the heart of all decision-making, eg who you promote, which projects get funding

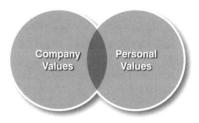

DOES IT MATTER?

At a recent conference focused on Generation Y, the panel of young people were asked who they would like to work for and, importantly, why.

Innocent Drinks – because they seem to treat their staff as real people and have a great deal of fun.

Virgin – because their values are very similar to mine: fun, value for money, quality, innovation, competitive challenge and brilliant customer service.

Google – they believe that if you focus on the user all else will follow. Other favourite values of theirs are: it's best to do one thing really, really well. You can make money without doing evil. You can be serious without a suit. Great just isn't good enough.

Astra Zeneca – because they appear to have total respect for their employees and take diversity seriously.

WL Gore – because they are passionate about being a great employer, they have a team orientation, and everyone has the same job title – associate.

PUT THE CUSTOMER AT THE HEART

BALANCED MEASURES

They say that what gets measured gets done. What does your organisation measure and share on a regular basis? Financials? Shareholder value? Make sure you have a few simple measures that indicate how effectively you are delivering excellent service.

For every measure, make sure that you have a target, ideally benchmarked against an aspirational external standard. Make sure also that you measure trends and, most importantly, that you actually use your measures to take action! For example:

- Customer complaints *give you* opportunities to improve
- Customer compliments *give you* opportunities to recognise great performance
- Lost customers *let you* get in touch and find out why
- Average duration of customer relationships *lets you* find out what keeps people loyal

Always check that the measures you reward are balanced. If you reward sales more than service, guess what your people will focus on.

> Did you know that Domino's train people to treat customers as though they are ordering a pizza worth $5000 because that's their lifetime value?

PUT THE CUSTOMER AT THE HEART

RECOGNITION AND REWARD

It's a natural human desire to be appreciated so remember to recognise, celebrate and reward your people. Here is a list to provoke ideas on how to put the customer at the heart of your approach to reward and recognition.

1. If you reward your sales people for **acquiring** customers, what do you do to recognise **creating loyal customers**?

2. How can you set up a scheme where colleagues can nominate each other for teamwork and service excellence?

3. How do you involve customers, or at least their feedback, in recognition?

4. When do you share customer complaints and compliments?

5. What processes do you have in place to recognise, on-the-spot, when someone has delivered exceptional service?

6. When you pay a bonus, increase someone's salary or simply recognise a job well done – do you always explain what has made the difference?

7. How well do you balance psychological and economic rewards, ie love or money?

PUT THE CUSTOMER AT THE HEART

COMMUNITY SERVICE

Your community, your customers! Successful organisations pay attention not just to employees and customers at work but also to the wider community. How is your organisation viewed in the community?

- Which local charities do you support?
- How do you get involved in local schools and hospitals?
- What sports and social activities do you support?
- How can you use your facilities, eg your training centre, to support your community?
- What skills and experience do you have that the community would value?

Whether you are a big corporation or an entrepreneur you can make a difference. What do you support and why?

Remember, it's not just money: you can give time or people too!

COACH FOR
BRILLIANT SERVICE

COACH FOR BRILLIANT SERVICE

FLATTENING THE PYRAMID

One of my favourite customer service books, *Moments of Truth*, was written by Jan Carlzon, then president of Scandinavian Airlines. Carlzon introduces the concept of flattening the pyramid: taking out the bureaucracy to give your employees the freedom to respond directly and quickly to customer needs.

Managing the situation – knowing what's going on, deciding what needs to be done and taking that action – has to be done as close to the customer as possible, ideally by the person in contact with the customer.

So, what does this mean for the traditional managers who believe that they are paid to be all-knowing and make the decisions?

FLATTENING THE PYRAMID

SERVICE TRIANGLE

The service manager has to have the mindset of **enabling** employees to deliver to the customer – **the mindset of a coach**.

You complete the triangle by positioning yourself where you can influence the performance of your people AND you can understand how they are performing in the eyes of the customer.

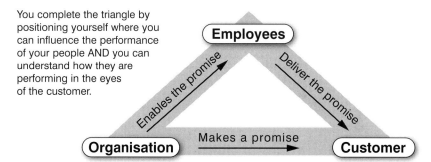

COACH FOR BRILLIANT SERVICE

WATCH THE GAME

As indicated by the service triangle, it is really important that, as a manager, you are in the game – both in terms of your people (players) and the customer (fans). You need to position yourself so that you can both coach your players and hear the fans. In the office, door closed, is probably the worst possible place to be.

Here are some suggestions to help you improve your ability to watch the game:

- Make yourself available to your team
- Ask what you can do to support your people
- Find out what is getting in the way of customer service
- Make sure that you hear and see the good stuff and the problems
- Be available to your customers and really listen
- Find out their preferences, understand wants and needs
- Explore ideas with your team and customers
- Make it simple for your customers to get in touch with you

FREEDOM TO ACT

Great service is not about rigid adherence to rules. You cannot create rules that deliver magic touches. Your behaviour as a manager creates the environment, the space, in which people feel confident to act with freedom, and that is when the magic happens! As they say at Virgin, *'you recruited them, so get on and trust them!'*

How often do you reflect on how your behaviour impacts on the actions of your people? These are some behaviours which encourage freedom to act:

- Let people know the boundaries of decision-making – what they can and should be responsible for – then trust them to do the best thing

- Encourage people to make mistakes, then learn from them so they don't make the same mistake twice

- Give people the opportunity to take responsibility for making decisions and acting on them – coach, don't tell

Continued… (71)

COACH FOR BRILLIANT SERVICE

FREEDOM TO ACT

- Actively seek and act on good ideas from other people
- Give recognition to people who strive to improve performance, not just your best people
- Display a 'can-do' attitude and a personal willingness to do things better
- Share customer feedback and ideas to inspire people to achieve more than they imagined possible
- Share stories where people have delivered magic touches
- Keep the promises you make to your people – go beyond their expectations when possible

COACH FOR BRILLIANT SERVICE

THE GIFT OF FEEDBACK

Well delivered and timely feedback to your people is the most powerful gift you have as a team leader. It creates a positive energy in others to either change what they do or, in the case of praise, do it again.

1. **Make sure you give feedback to your people every day**
    Often, managers forget or avoid giving feedback and it invariably leads to employees, good or otherwise, gradually withdrawing commitment and, ultimately, to 'extinction'.

2. **Catch people doing things right**
    A good rule of thumb is to reinforce the right behaviour three times more frequently than picking up on the wrong behaviour. Don't always feel, however, that you have to sandwich negative feedback between praise. Say it as it is so that your employees hear the real message – don't hide it.

Continued... (73)

THE GIFT OF FEEDBACK

3. **Go for the ball not the player**
   When you give tough feedback make sure that you focus on tackling the shortfall in performance rather than the personality of the individual.

4. **Shine the light**
   You hold the torch of feedback so think carefully about where you decide to shine the light. Use your expertise to focus your feedback and coaching on what will make the most difference to an individual's performance.

5. **Hold up the mirror**
   Ask questions that get people to accurately assess how they are doing. You hold the mirror, they describe what they see.

6. **Start with yourself**
   Ask for feedback from your own people on how you are doing. Show you are willing to listen, act and improve. Others will follow your lead.

CUSTOMER CONTACT
COACHING EXAMPLE

Almost every set of customer service standards will include an expectation about the nature of the contact with the customer. For example: '*Be friendly*'.

So, how can you use the lessons in coaching and feedback to get people to improve how they perform?

1. **Describe** what is expected and what isn't
2. **Reflect** on what actually happens
3. Provide specific **feedback**
4. Change **perspective**

We will look at this in more detail.

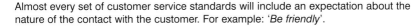

CUSTOMER CONTACT

1. **Describe**
   Describe what each standard means in practice or, even better, get people to describe it to you. For example:

   Be friendly – *show warmth, make eye contact, smile and make a positive impression but never, ever force it!*

2. **Reflect**
   Now, use your coaching skills to shine the light on the standards by using good questions:

   How did you come across to the customer?

   What did you do to create a positive impression?

   What response did you get from the customer?

   What could you do differently (or the same) to create a real connection?

CUSTOMER CONTACT

3. **Feedback**

   Ask questions to generate specific and measurable feedback. Encourage people to set targets for themselves:

   How many customers did you greet in the last hour?

   How many did you make direct eye contact with?

   What would make it easier for you?

   How did the customers respond when you made eye contact?

4. **Perspective**

   Finally, create an opportunity for people to see things through the customer's eyes.

   If I asked your last customer about the impression you created, what would they say?
   Actually find a customer and ask them!

COACH FOR BRILLIANT SERVICE

WHEN PERFORMANCE FALTERS

Even the best people can be stopped in their tracks by lazy managers. If your people aren't performing as expected, then first look at the things within your control. Use this checklist to identify what action will make the difference.

Task clarity	Do your people know what *good* looks like?
Task priority	Do they understand the impact of what they are doing?
Competence	Do your people have the skills to do the job?
Obstacles	What are the real or imagined procedural barriers (rules) that are getting in the way?
Reward for failure	Do your decisions reward the wrong behaviour?
Performance feedback	Are you providing consistent and timely feedback on how your people are doing?
Role/person mismatch	Is the person in the right job or team?
OK, they are being wilful!	Consider formal performance management

BE CONTAGIOUS

Attitude is infectious! As the famous quote goes, '*you have to be the change you want to see in others*'. Like it or not, what you do rubs off on others.

How you behave is driven, ultimately, by the skills you have developed but more importantly by the beliefs and values you hold.

- Do you believe that it is your role to support your people?

- Do you believe that you have to deliver what you promise to your own employees?

- Do you believe that everyone is equal in the eyes of the customer?

GETTING YOUR PEOPLE TOGETHER

We've already written about flattening the pyramid (page 68) so that your people, those closest to the customer, can make the best decision for the customer. As the manager you cannot be there all the time. That said, you will normally have at least two chances to coach your people, before and after they come into contact with the customer. In most sports, the coach also has the opportunity to have a half-time team talk to make small adjustments to the game plan.

What are your opportunities to coach the team?

When it really matters, roll up your sleeves and help out your team – the ability to practise what you preach can speak volumes!

COACH FOR BRILLIANT SERVICE

OFF TO A FLYING START

What do you do to get your people really focused on the customer before the day (or night) begins?

Here is a list to stimulate ideas about how you can use this valuable time:

- Clarify the individual roles each person in the team needs to fulfil – the game plan!

- Check everyone understands changes to product or service

- Share what you know about today's customers. How can you use that information?

- Agree the targets for the shift. What will make it a success?

- Ask what you can do to perform even better than yesterday

Continued…

COACH FOR BRILLIANT SERVICE

OFF TO A FLYING START

- Plan how to get your best people in the key roles

- Position your 'learners' so that they can learn from the best and feel confident in what you have asked them to do

- Agree the service basics you want people to focus on

- Predict and rehearse the difficult situations ahead

- Talk about where the pressure is likely to be on this shift

- Take the opportunity to recognise recent exceptional performance

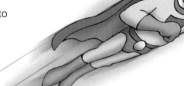

WRAP IT UP

The end of the shift/day is an equally important opportunity to engage with your people. Here are some ideas on how you can use this valuable time:

- Celebrate success
- Discuss ideas your people have to improve for next time
- Agree what didn't go to plan and what you can learn from this
- Find a way to remind people of what is most important to the customer
- Start to prepare for the next time
- Identify what information you can pass on to another team to help them
- Look for something funny or light-hearted to share so you can end the day with a smile

Take five minutes to ask each of your people:

- What was your score out of 10 today?
- What successes did you have?
- What would have made it a 10?

Act now to get it right tomorrow!

BECOME A FANTASTIC STORY TELLER

You can't define excellence – it just happens. No amount of rules will inspire people to perform at an exceptional level. You have to learn to tell stories!

Story telling, ever since humans sat round the camp fire, has been the way to pass on information about boundaries, values and beliefs. It is through sharing stories that you can inspire people towards the art of the possible.

Think about your 'legends' of customer service. What are your organisation's stories of excellence? Pick stories that:

- Describe your organisation's values at their best, eg creativity, problem-solving
- Let your people know what you believe to be great
- Are aspirational but possible
- Can be easily remembered and retold
- Have a positive ending for the customer

COACH FOR BRILLIANT SERVICE

PASSING THE BALL THROUGH OTHERS

Who in your organisation is responsible for customer service? The answer in great organisations is always **everyone**!

At Disney the story is that everyone has the title 'Manager, Customer Relations' on their business card.

At Virgin Atlantic they have a fantastic internal video about what it takes to get an aircraft departing on time. The final credits list all the people involved – you've guessed it, the credits list everyone in the airline.

COACH FOR BRILLIANT SERVICE

PASSING THE BALL THROUGH OTHERS

The analogy of passing the ball to someone else in your team gets across the role we all have in delivering to someone else. Who do you rely on to give you the perfectly weighted pass? Who relies on you?

In great companies people try to provide the perfect pass to colleagues so that it is really easy to use and pass on to others. Great people look beyond the next person and care about passing the ball **through** others.

Think outside of your team – think BIG picture!

Use the questionnaire on the opposite page to assess how well your team passes the ball through others. If you score 5 or more you are doing well. What will it take to get your score to 10/10?

COACH FOR BRILLIANT SERVICE

PASSING THE BALL THROUGH OTHERS
QUESTIONNAIRE

	Yes	No
1. We know the players (departments) we must pass the ball to regularly.	☐	☐
2. We can describe the quality of pass we need to make (because we've asked or observed them!).	☐	☐
3. We can consistently pass the ball to this standard.	☐	☐
4. We are aware of how the other players will use the ball.	☐	☐
5. We get feedback on how well we have passed the ball.	☐	☐
6. We get feedback on how well the other player has used the pass we made (did they score?).	☐	☐
7. We actively ask for ideas on how we could improve the quality of the pass we make.	☐	☐
8. We recognise and reward 'assists' not just the goals.	☐	☐
9. We are agile enough to quickly adapt the pass we make to others when the game changes.	☐	☐
10. We have shared all of the above (1-9) with others who **we** rely on…..we don't wait to be asked.	☐	☐

COACH FOR BRILLIANT SERVICE

EVERY TOUCH MATTERS

Another belief that prevails in great service organisations is that 'every touch matters'. Much is written about identifying *moments of truth* – knowing the critical moments that the customer will notice and value.

Is it possible to switch excellence on and off?

We would recommend you as coach to encourage your people to treat every contact with customers or colleagues as if it is the most important.

Ask your people to take it one customer at a time ....make each customer feel unique.

COACH FOR BRILLIANT SERVICE

TURNAROUND

Here is a simple exercise to complete when service standards are not as you expect.
Get your team together and ask them to write down what they personally expect as a
customer. You can get them started with the statement:

As a customer I expect .....

They may list things like:

● I should get full and undivided attention

● The people I deal with should be competent and knowledgeable

Then turn the list around and ask how your organisation's service compares with this list.
What are the good and bad examples of service? What is the impact on the customer
and your business? What can you learn?

Ask each of them to commit to one immediate change to improve what they do.

COACH FOR BRILLIANT SERVICE

POSITIVE MENTAL ATTITUDE

People who provide excellent customer service always have the right attitude – a positive attitude!

At recruitment it's really important that you listen for attitude. If you can't spot it in the interview then think about introducing job previews where you can watch your potential recruits in practice.

How do they treat each other when the customers aren't around – does the mask quickly slip? Try and pick people who are happy on the inside.

POSITIVE MENTAL ATTITUDE

Negative attitude

Customers are always moaning

My colleagues just don't pull their weight

Customers can never make up their minds

Positive attitude

Feedback is always valuable

What can I do to help my colleagues get better at what they do?

How can I help the customer understand the choices they have?

As coach, it is your role to hold up the mirror and let people know which attitude is on show. Customers can be frustrating and even the best employee has to let off steam, so make sure you create that safety valve for your people. Just do it in private and get people positive before it drifts into something more chronic.

COACH FOR BRILLIANT SERVICE

POLAROID PICTURE

I acknowledge my thanks to Frank Dick, OBE who introduced me to the mindset of being the **best that you can be**. Here is a simple exercise to help people understand what this means.

If you took a photograph of yourself at the end of the day would you be proud enough to sign it to say.......that's been me at my best today?

Buy a Polaroid camera and ask your team to take photographs of each other. Ask them if they are happy to sign the photo – if yes, get them to write down their answers to the following questions.

1. What did I do for our customers today that made me proud?
2. What did I do for my colleagues today that made me proud?
3. What can I learn from today that will make me even better next time?

> Excellence is an art won by training and habituation...We are what we repeatedly do. Excellence then, is not an act but a habit.
>
> **Aristotle**

CREATE THE FREEDOM TO IMPROVE

CREATE THE FREEDOM TO IMPROVE

THE BEST THAT YOU CAN BE!

As a manager you have to create an environment where people have the freedom to improve. What you have to do is:

- Help employees bounce back when things haven't gone to plan

- Encourage people to do things that little bit better

- Get your team striving for more radical innovation to improve the customer experience

- Encourage people to share experiences and learn from each other

CREATE THE FREEDOM TO IMPROVE

BOUNCE BACK

How do your people bounce back when things don't go as planned? Your ability to recover when you don't meet customer expectations can actually drive customer loyalty. A few simple tips can make all the difference.

Have the courtesy to say sorry
Accept the fact that, in the eyes of the customer, you have failed to meet expectations and it is **your** responsibility, on behalf of your company. Get on and make a quick and sincere apology.

Fix it quick – no questions
As a minimum you have to rectify the situation or let the customer know what you'll do to achieve this. If the solution will take time then keep the customer informed. Never tell the customer what you can't do unless it is immediately followed by a description of what you can do for them.

Show empathy
Listen carefully and put yourself in the customer's shoes – you know how they feel. Diffuse the emotion by letting people know that you understand their feelings.

Continued… (95)

BOUNCE BACK

You have one chance so take it
Everyone makes mistakes and most reasonable customers will give you one chance to put it right – make sure that you take it! Breaking promises during service recovery has a deadly impact on customer loyalty.

Leave the customer better off than before
Put it right and more – find a creative way to reach a resolution and, ideally, let your people make the decision about what is the right way to put it right – they are closest to the emotion.

Book in a check-up
Thank the customer for the opportunity to put the matter right and make contact later to check that it really has been resolved fully.

The customer is **not** always right, but you should never go out of your way to prove them wrong.

CREATE THE FREEDOM TO IMPROVE

CUSTOMER CHARTER

What is your customer charter? Are you confident that your employees understand and act on it?

Here is an example of one organisation's customer charter.

We solemnly pledge......

- *To respect customers and be friendly towards them*
- *To design our processes and products to be easy and good value for our customers*
- *To give a grumbling customer the benefit of the doubt and treat their complaints sympathetically*
- *To acknowledge written complaints within 7 days*
- *To respond in full to written complaints within 21 days*
- *To respond to phone calls and emails within 48 hours*
- *To ensure our responses are accurate, error free and honest*
- *To give compensation where compensation is due*

CREATE THE FREEDOM TO IMPROVE

CUSTOMER CHARTER

How does your organisation treat customer feedback? Here are some examples:

Invite feedback (Virgin)
Today's customer complaint could be tomorrow's million pound business idea.
All feedback should be recorded, reviewed and acted upon.

Feedback can be fun (Innocent)
Three Cambridge graduates had a business idea. To test their idea they experimented with recipes and then booked a stall at a jazz festival, bought £500 worth of fruit and turned it into smoothies to sell. They put up a notice, asking their customers if they should give up their jobs and concentrate on making smoothies full time, and provided 'Yes' and 'No' litter bins. By the end of the festival the bin marked 'Yes' was overflowing. They all quit the next day......and founded the successful Innocent Drinks.

Act quickly (Costa Coffee)
Give us your feedback so that we can do it better tomorrow!

INVITE feedback, make it FUN and ACT ON IT!

CREATE THE FREEDOM TO IMPROVE

PUTTING ON THE EARS

Disney has a wonderful phrase to help employees understand the importance of listening to the customer informally: *putting on the ears*. Everyone, regardless of job title, has to put on the ears and listen to the customer.

There are many ways that you can organise your customer feedback:

- Balance formal and informal methods
- Pool the feedback and look for common themes
- Develop methods that involve a cross-section of your people
- Pay equal attention to complaints and compliments
- Share customer feedback widely
- Always thank people for feedback and act wherever possible

FEEDBACK METHODS

Here are some ways of getting feedback which you may decide to put in place.

	Informal	Formal
Act later	• Surveys – with added entertainment factor, eg Innocent • 'Back to the floor' activities • Mystery shoppers • Blogs	• Longer-term changes – trends • Demographic research, eg Generation Y
Act now	• Listen in, ie put on the ears • Talk to customers • Temperature checks	• Feedback cards • Complimentary letters • Written complaints • Online contact

CREATE THE FREEDOM TO IMPROVE

ONE STEP BEYOND

It's the little things that count.

Use the creative power of your people to generate ideas that will improve the customer experience – little by little! Your people are, after all, that little bit closer to the customer than you.

- At the end of the shift ask your employees what they could do differently to make the customer experience even better

- Ask your people what gets in the way of delivering excellent service

- Invite some of your team to experience the service as a customer and write down what they noticed – was it as expected?

- Think about any great service you have received in the last week – how could you replicate the experience in your own organisation

- Ask your employees to comment on their experience of the competition: what they do well and what they don't

However you generate the ideas, write them down and implement at least one a week – the difference will soon add up!

CREATE THE FREEDOM TO IMPROVE

MYSTERY SHOPPERS

Mystery shoppers can be a great way to test the customer experience. To get the most value from the activity, follow the advice below:

- Make sure that you have defined the service standards expected of your people and shared them with your employees – it's only fair!

- Ask your mystery shoppers to test the service not just product, process or sales techniques

- Ask for a commentary on what actually happened, not just tick boxes. For example, ask them how they felt, who stood out and what happened that wasn't on the checklist, eg magic touches

- Think about asking your mystery shoppers to talk to your people and/or in customer service training

COMPETITORS

Do yesterday what your competitors will strive to do tomorrow

It may feel like a battle for the customer but never, ever knock your competitors. Instead, admire and appreciate what they achieve and can do, and learn from them. Talk to those of your team who have worked elsewhere, to get new ideas.

Who are your competitors?

If you want to be a leading service brand then you have to look beyond your direct competition and compare yourself with every other service brand, otherwise you will suffer by comparison. Anyone who strives to raise customer expectations – supermarkets, insurance companies, airlines, hotels – effectively raises expectations for you. For example, the 'no quibble' returns policy at Marks & Spencer has raised expectations for everyone.

CREATE THE FREEDOM TO IMPROVE

WHAT IF....?

Simply asking the customer what they want or need can be a limiting way to improve the service experience. You need imagination to introduce the art of the possible!

The secret of success is the ability to put yourself in another person's shoes and consider things from his or her point of view as well as your own.

Then use your imagination to explore what could be done. This may require you to suspend some of the usual barriers to thinking that can get in the way of great ideas, eg no money, no space, no time, etc.

Cast your mind forward to a different place, eg 2050, and explore what the future may bring.

Also think beyond your direct competition for ideas. The McDonalds drive-thru was the inspiration for the Virgin Atlantic drive-thru that has significantly accelerated the check-in times for Upper Class customers.

DESIGNING FROM INSIDE THE CUSTOMER'S HEAD

At Virgin they look for insights into what the customer really wants.

Observation	Innovation
Everyone loves eating ice cream at the cinema	Why not offer an ice cream to airline passengers when they are watching movies on board the aircraft
There is nothing worse than looking at the back of someone's seat for 8 hours	Why not fit a TV on the back of every seat on the plane?
The biggest problem with taking kids by train rather than by car is the embarrassment when they get bored and start running up and down the carriage	Why not introduce activity packs for kids on all trains?
What is the song they are playing in the shop (you don't want to look uncool by asking?)	Let's introduce the first ever national, in-store radio station into Virgin Megastores

CREATE THE FREEDOM TO IMPROVE

KEEP MOVING

Once you think that you have cracked it, think again.

- Keep on thinking of ideas that add value – make a difference

- Keep on making things even simpler – customers love clever simplicity

- Keep on challenging the norm – are you sure the rules are real?

- Keep on learning from your mistakes – but try not to make the same one twice

- Keep moving – but never change for change's sake!

Good Luck!

USEFUL INFORMATION

FURTHER READING & REFERENCES

I've been influenced by many people, many organisations and many books. Here are some books that are well worth a read.

Customer Loyalty: A Guide for Time Travellers, Sionade Robinson & Lyn Etherington, Palgrave MacMillan, 2005

Moments of Truth: New Strategies for Today's Customer Driven Economy, Jan Carlzon, Harper Collins, 1989

Managing the Customer Experience: Turning Customers into Advocates, Shaun Smith & Joe Wheeler, FT Prentice Hall, 2002

Inside the Magic Kingdom – Seven Keys to Disney's Success, Tom Connellan, Bard Press, 1997

The Richer Way, Julian Ritcher, Emap Business Communications, 2001

Fish – a Remarkable Way to Boost Morale and Improve Results, S Lundin, H Paul & J Christensen, Hodder & Stoughton, 2002

What Customers Like About You – Adding Emotional Value for Service Excellence and Competitive Advantage, David Freemantle, Nicholas Brealey Publishing, 1999

The Loyalty Effect – the Hidden Force Behind Growth, Profits and Lasting Value, F Reichheld, Harvard Business School Press, 1996

These titles are also published by Management Pocketbooks.

THE MANAGEMENT POCKETBOOK SERIES

Pocketbooks

360 Degree Feedback
Appraisals
Assertiveness
Balance Sheet
Business Planning
Business Writing
Call Centre Customer Care
Career Transition
Coaching
Communicator's
Competencies
Controlling Absenteeism
Creative Manager's
C.R.M.
Cross-cultural Business
Customer Service
Decision-making
Delegation
Developing People
Discipline
Diversity
E-commerce
Emotional Intelligence
Employment Law
Empowerment

Energy and Well-being
Facilitator's
Flexible Workplace
Handling Complaints
Icebreakers
Impact & Presence
Improving Efficiency
Improving Profitability
Induction
Influencing
International Trade
Interviewer's
I.T. Trainer's
Key Account Manager's
Leadership
Learner's
Manager's
Managing Budgets
Managing Cashflow
Managing Change
Managing Customer Service
Managing Difficult Participants
Managing Recruitment
Managing Upwards
Managing Your Appraisal

Marketing
Meetings
Mentoring
Motivation
Negotiator's
Networking
NLP
Openers & Closers
People Manager's
Performance Management
Personal Success
Positive Mental Attitude
Presentations
Problem Behaviour
Problem Solving
Project Management
Psychometric Testing
Resolving Conflict
Reward
Sales Excellence
Salesperson's
Self-managed Development
Starting In Management
Strategy
Stress

Succeeding at Interviews
Talent Management
Teambuilding Activities
Teamworking
Telephone Skills
Telesales
Thinker's
Time Management
Trainer Standards
Trainer's
Training Evaluation
Training Needs Analysis
Virtual Teams
Vocal Skills
Workplace Politics

Pocketfiles

Trainer's Blue Pocketfile of
Ready-to-use Activities

Trainer's Green Pocketfile of
Ready-to-use Activities

Trainer's Red Pocketfile of
Ready-to-use Activities

19.06.08

About the Author

Andy Cross

Andy is Head of Organisation and People Development at
Virgin Atlantic. With a diverse background in financial services,
customer services and consultancy, Andy loves sharing ideas with
others and helping people, teams and organisations to perform.

Andy's passion for growing talent extends to his love of his
family and sport – trying to keep up with the kids and to
slow down the transition from player of many sports to
coach of a few.

Contact

Andy can be contacted at Virgin Atlantic or email andycross@ntlworld.com
83 Somerset Road
Meadvale
Reigate
RH1 6ND

ORDER FORM

	No. copies

Your details

Name _____

Position _____

Company _____

Address _____

_____

_____

Telephone _____

Fax _____

E-mail _____

VAT No. (EC companies) _____

Your Order Ref _____

Please send me:

The <u>Managing Customer Service</u> Pocketbook ▢

The _____ Pocketbook ▢

The _____ Pocketbook ▢

The _____ Pocketbook ▢

Order by Post

MANAGEMENT POCKETBOOKS LTD

LAUREL HOUSE, STATION APPROACH,
ALRESFORD, HAMPSHIRE SO24 9JH UK

Order by Phone, Fax or Internet
Telephone: +44 (0)1962 735573
Facsimile: +44 (0)1962 733637
E-mail: sales@pocketbook.co.uk
Web: www.pocketbook.co.uk

Customers in USA should contact:
Management Pocketbooks
2427 Bond Street, University Park, IL 60466
Telephone: 866 620 6944 Facsimile: 708 534 7803
E-mail: mp.orders@ware-pak.com
Web: www.managementpocketbooks.com